Unheard

Lament for Solo Viola

Xavier Hersom

Program Note

The viola is an undervalued instrument that has the incredible ability to portray deep emotional music. I composed the lament "Unheard" for solo viola to address those whose culture, stories, history, and music remain unheard within society.

Performance Note

This solo explores the diversity of tone and color capable of the viola. The performer should pay special attention to accents and articulations and prepare to quickly navigate between the instrument's upper and lower ranges.

Duration: ca. 3'10"
Grades 4-5

Unheared
Lament for Solo Viola

Xavier Hersom

Score

©2023

33
With Emotion!
ff
37
Flowing
fff
ff
39
f
43
ff
Stately
fff
f
rit. Lament
47
(♩ = 65)
mp
52
molto rit.
mf
p
ppp

Listen to a recording here:

About the Composer

Xavier Hersom (b.1995) is an international-award-winning transgender composer. Though influenced by tonal music of the Romantic period, Hersom's compositions are inspired by current national issues. He believes art enables people to see the world from other perspectives and that music can spread awareness of social injustices. Learn more about him at:

www.XavierHersom.com

If you enjoy this music, please consider leaving a review.

Thank you!

www.ingramcontent.com/pod-product-compliance
Lightning Source LLC
Chambersburg PA
CBHW081454070426
42452CB00042B/2729